DISCARD

D1470465

Miracle mug cakes

and other cheat's bakes

Miracle mug cakes

and other cheat's bakes

28 quick and easy recipes for tasty treats

SUZY PELTA

photography by
ADRIAN LAWRENCE

RYLAND PETERS & SMALL
LONDON • NEW YORK

For Tal, Louis, Gracie and Amelie

Author acknowledgments:
Huge thanks must go to Adrian Lawrence, Luis Peral and Sian Henley for making my recipes look so delicious. To Cindy Richards, Julia Charles, Stephanie Milner, Leslie Harrington, Toni Kay and Gordana Simakovic at Ryland Peters and Small for producing this beautiful book and for believing in baking that is unashamedly trashy. To my agent and friend Anne Kibel, for way too many reasons to fit into a paragraph. To my family, including my brilliant sister Caz-bar, who are my biggest supporters. Special mention to my very brave and inspirational Mum and Dad (see Dad you got a mention!). To all of my fantastic friends, especially chief taster Natasha and chief non-taster Hayley – I couldn't have done this without you both. And to my incredible Tal, Louis, Gracie and Amelie, I love you all so much and this book truly is for you.

Senior designer Toni Kay
Commissioning editor Stephanie Milner
Production Manager Gordana Simakovic
Art director Leslie Harrington
Editorial director Julia Charles
Publisher Cindy Richards

Food stylist Sian Henley
Prop stylist and art direction Luis Peral
Indexer Vanessa Bird

First published in 2017 by
Ryland Peters and Small
20–21 Jockey's Fields
London WC1R 4BW
and
341 E 116th St
New York NY 10029
www.rylandpeters.com

10 9 8 7 6 5 4 3 2 1

Text copyright © Suzy Pelta 2017

Design and photographs copyright
© Ryland Peters & Small 2017

ISBN: 978-1-84975-812-3

Printed in China

A CIP record for this book is available from the British Library.

US Library of Congress Cataloging-in-Publication Data has been applied for.

NOTES:
• Both British (Metric) and American (Imperial plus US cups) measurements are included in these recipes for convenience; however it is important to work with one set of measurements and not alternate between the two within a recipe.
• All spoon measurements are level unless otherwise specified.
• UK medium eggs are of equivalent size to US large and UK large to US extra-large. Uncooked or partially cooked eggs should not be served to the very old, frail, young children, pregnant women or those with compromised immune systems.
• Ovens should be preheated to the specified temperatures. We recommend using an oven thermometer. If using a fan-assisted oven, adjust temperatures according to the manufacturer's instructions.
• When a recipe calls for the grated zest of citrus fruit, buy unwaxed fruit and wash well before using. If you can only find treated fruit, scrub well in warm soapy water before using.
• There are certain health risks associated with whipped cream so always practise food safety by using fresh cream before its expiry date and covering and storing prepared desserts in the refrigerator until ready to serve.

Contents

Introduction 6

Mug cakes for kids 8

Mug cakes for grown-ups 16

Mug cakes for family fun 26

Cookie cheats 34

Cheat's cakes and desserts 44

No-bake bakes 54

Index 64

Introduction

Lets face it; sometimes you really just need cake and usually it's when there isn't any in the house. The weather is miserable outside, your tummy is rumbling and the calls from your sweet tooth need answering swiftly.

This is where you need mug cakes in your life. In this, my first recipe book, I want to show you everything that is right with these miracle mug cakes. Using mostly store-cupboard ingredients and a microwave, in just a few minutes you can have cake ready to eat, and delicious, moist, flavoursome cake at that.

Ok, so they're not the most refined form of baking, yes they are made in a microwave, but you know what? You can fill your tummy and fill your home with the smells of baking without a lot of effort!

Baking really should be all about having fun, whether you are baking with children, or perhaps like me, you are also a big kid at heart! I believe the baking rules are there to be broken, and if that means using a few short-cuts or 'cheats' then why not? We all lead such busy and hectic lives, so allow yourself to take a few helping hands, such as store-bought puff pastry or even a boxed cake mix. The end product will still be scrumptious and made with love; it just won't have taken as much time!

So whether you are looking for a cake-fix in a mug (even one with a cheeky drop of alcohol), an easy cookie, a speedy but yummy dessert or a straightforward no-bake recipe, there is something for you here. Beginners should find recipes that they can make with their eyes shut (almost) and advanced bakers will be grateful for a day off from anything too complicated!

HINTS AND TIPS FOR MAKING MUG CAKES

• In the same way that you know your oven, get to know your microwave. All of the baking times here are based on using an 800W microwave, so adjust the times if your microwave is more or less powerful.

• Mug cakes bake in the microwave and therefore will have a different texture to a cake baked in an oven. They taste more like a steamed pudding and will never get a brown or crisp top. For the best eating experience they should generally be enjoyed soon after they are out of the microwave as they can dry out quickly.

• Where eggs are used in mug cakes they should always be at room temperature.

• Use the largest microwave-safe mug that you have to make your mug cakes and place the mug on a plate in the microwave to catch any possible spills. Especially note the recipes where I have mentioned a large mug as these recipes will have a larger batter and will rise a lot!

• Mug cakes will rise and then deflate when the microwave door opens. This is normal. When a mug cake is fully baked it will have risen, started to come away from the sides of the mug and will be slightly damp to the touch.

• Often batter will run down the sides of the mug while baking in the microwave. Mug cakes dry out very quickly once cooked, so the wetter the batter and the damper the cake when it comes out of the microwave, the better the taste experience and the longer it will stay moist.

Mug cakes for kids

PB-Nutella mug cake

PREPARE: **2 MINUTES** MICROWAVE: **1 MINUTE 40 SECONDS** COOL: **2 MINUTES**

2 tablespoons vegetable oil
1 UK medium/US large egg
2 tablespoons caster/
  granulated sugar
3 tablespoons self-raising/
  rising flour
a pinch of salt
2 tablespoons smooth
  peanut butter
2 tablespoons Nutella

a large microwavable mug

MAKES 1

Nutella and peanut butter are a marriage made in mug cake heaven! Not only is the sponge a sweet, salty and nutty delight, but there is also a pool of warm Nutella and peanut butter at the bottom. Just gorgeous!

Using a fork, beat together the vegetable oil and egg in a mug.

Add the sugar and mix thoroughly.

Pour in the flour and salt, and mix well until you have a smooth batter.

Add 1 tablespoon of the peanut butter and 1 tablespoon of the Nutella into the mixture and stir until they are both fully combined.

Drop the remaining peanut butter and Nutella on top of the mixture, along with 1 teaspoon of water, but do not mix them in.

Microwave for 1 minute 40 seconds at 800W. The cake will rise, and should still be quite wet to touch. (It also may well drip a little down the sides of the mug as it is such a moist batter).

Leave the mug cake to cool for 2 minutes before eating, then devour.

Sprinkle sunshine mug cake

PREPARE: 2 MINUTES MICROWAVE: **1 MINUTES 50 SECONDS** COOL: **2 MINUTES**

2 tablespoons unsalted butter

25 g/1 oz. white chocolate, chopped into small pieces

1 tablespoon whole milk

1 teaspoon vanilla extract

1 UK medium/US large egg

2 tablespoons caster/ granulated sugar

4 tablespoons self-raising/ rising flour

1 tablespoon confetti-style cake sprinkles (pictured page 6)

TO SERVE

vanilla frosting

cake sprinkles

a large microwavable mug

MAKES 1

A soft moist vanilla mug cake overloaded with sprinkles is a delight for children – big and small. Make sure you use confetti sprinkles as their colour doesn't run into the batter. For an extra treat, top with store-bought vanilla frosting and lots more sprinkles.

Put the butter and white chocolate into a large mug and microwave at 800W for 20–30 seconds until the chocolate has melted.

Stir the melted chocolate and butter together. Add the milk and vanilla, and stir again until smooth.

Using a fork, beat in the egg until fully combined.

Add in the sugar and stir thoroughly.

Pour in the flour and mix well until you have a smooth batter.

Carefully fold the sprinkles into the batter.

Microwave for 1 minute 50 seconds at 800W. The cake will rise, then sink a little and should still be quite wet to touch. (It also may well drip a little down the sides of the mug as it is such a moist batter).

Leave the mug cake to cool for 2 minutes. Top with store-bought vanilla frosting and extra sprinkles before eating.

Cookie dough mug cake

PREPARE: **2 MINUTES** MICROWAVE: **50 SECONDS** COOL: **5 MINUTES**

All the deliciousness of cookie dough baked in under a minute in your microwave. Top with your favourite ice cream and crushed Oreos for dessert heaven!

In a small bowl, cream together the butter and both sugars using the back of a spoon.

Add the egg yolk and stir until fully combined.

Pour in the vanilla and mix again.

Add the flour and salt, and stir, before using your hands to bring the dough together.

Add the chocolate chips and make sure they are evenly incorporated.

Put the dough in the ramekin or small mug and push down so that it has a flat top.

Pour the milk over the top of the unbaked cookie dough mug cake and swirl it around so it covers the entire surface.

Put the ramekin or mug on a shallow bowl or plate (to catch any excess milk) and microwave for 50 seconds at 800W. If there is still a little milk on top after microwaving, pour it away.

Leave the cookie dough to cool for 5 minutes before topping with your favourite ice cream and crumble over a little cookie, then enjoy.

NOTE: Mug cakes are best eaten soon after they are made but if you leave this mug cake to cool a little, it will form a firmer cookie at the bottom.

1 tablespoon unsalted butter, at room temperature
1 tablespoon caster/ granulated sugar
1 tablespoon light brown sugar
1 UK medium/US large egg yolk
1 teaspoon vanilla extract
5 tablespoons plain/all-purpose flour
a pinch of salt
1 tablespoon milk/semi-sweet chocolate chips
1 teaspoon whole milk

TO SERVE
ice cream or whipped cream
crushed Oreo cookies

a ramekin or small microwavable mug

MAKES 1

Oreo mug cake

PREPARE: **2 MINUTES** MICROWAVE: **1 MINUTE 20 SECONDS** COOL: **3 MINUTES**

2 tablespoons unsalted butter
35 g/1¹/₄ oz. milk/semi-sweet
   chocolate chips
2 tablespoons caster/
   granulated sugar
1 UK medium/US large egg
3 tablespoons self-raising/
   rising flour
2–3 Oreo cookies
whipped cream, to serve
   (optional)

a large microwavable mug

MAKES 1

This soft chocolate sponge has a delightful surprise hidden inside it – two Oreo cookies! Make sure you push the Oreos into the batter, so you can choose whether to hint at the cookie centre with an extra one on top or keep it a surprise!

Add the butter and chocolate chips to a large mug and microwave for 20–30 seconds until the chocolate has melted.

Stir the melted chocolate and butter to combine. Add the sugar and stir again.

Using a fork, beat in the egg until fully combined.

Add in the flour and mix thoroughly until you have a smooth batter – checking that there is no unmixed flour at the bottom of the mug.

Carefully drop two of the cookies into the mug, one on top of the other, making sure that they are fully covered by cake mixture.

Microwave for 1 minute 20 seconds at 800W. The cake will rise, then sink a little and should still be quite wet to touch.

Leave the mug cake to cool for 3 minutes, then top with whipped cream and poke in an extra cookie, if desired. Enjoy right away.

Boozy berry mug cake

PREPARE: **2 MINUTES** MICROWAVE: **1 MINUTE 50 SECONDS** COOL: **3 MINUTES**

2 tablespoons unsalted butter
1 teaspoon vanilla extract
1 UK medium/US large egg
2 tablespoons caster/
    granulated sugar
5 tablespoons self-raising/
    rising flour
2 tablespoons raspberry jam/
    jelly
1 tablespoon brandy

TO SERVE
jam/jelly
whipped cream
fresh fruit

a microwavable mug

MAKES 1

Fruit preserves swirled into a soft brandy-topped sponge makes the most warming, comforting and sweet mug cake. It is literally a hug in a mug!

Put the butter into the mug and microwave for 20–30 seconds at 800W until melted.

Stir in the vanilla, then, using a fork, beat in the egg until fully combined.

Add the sugar and stir thoroughly.

Pour in the flour and mix thoroughly until you have a thick cake batter.

Temporarily remove a couple of spoonfuls of the mixture into a separate bowl.

Drop the jam/jelly on top of the mixture in the mug and using a fork, gently swirl it in, before pouring the brandy over the top.

Empty the mixture that was in the separate bowl over the top. (The brandy will still be quite liquid on top, so carefully smooth the batter so that the jam is covered.)

Put the mug on a plate and microwave for 1 minute 50 seconds at 800W. The cake will rise and then sink a little and should still be a little wet to touch. (You should place it on a plate in case any of the jam/jelly leaks.)

Leave the mug cake to cool for 3 minutes before spreading with a little extra jam/jelly and topping with a swirl of whipped cream. I like to adorn mine with fresh raspberries or other fresh fruit to match the flavour of the jam/jelly. Be careful when eating as the jam/jelly centre will still be quite hot.

2 tablespoons unsalted butter

60 g/2 oz. white chocolate

zest of 1/2 lemon

2 tablespoons caster/
granulated sugar

1 UK medium/US large egg

4 tablespoons self-raising/
rising flour

1 tablespoon almond liqueur,
to serve (optional)

LEMON DRIZZLE

freshly squeezed juice of
1/2 lemon

1 tablespoon icing/
confectioners' sugar

a microwavable mug

MAKES 1

White chocolate and lemon drizzle mug cake

PREPARE: **2 MINUTES**   MICROWAVE: **1 MINUTE 40 SECONDS**   COOL: **3 MINUTES**

Creamy white chocolate at the bottom of the mug with a lemon drizzle on top takes this mug cake to another level of deliciousness. Add in the almond liqueur if you're feeling especially cheeky!

Chop 40 g/1½ oz. of the white chocolate into small pieces and along with the butter, add it to a mug. Microwave for 20–30 seconds at 800W until the chocolate has melted. Set the remaining chocolate aside.

Stir the melted chocolate and butter, add the lemon zest and stir again.

Add the sugar and mix thoroughly.

Using a fork, beat in the egg until fully combined.

Empty in the flour and mix well until you have a smooth batter.

Drop the remaining chocolate into the mixture, along with 1 teaspoon of water.

Microwave for 1 minute 40 seconds at 800W. The cake will rise, and should still be quite wet to touch. (It also may well drip a little down the sides of the mug as it is such a moist batter.)

While the mug cake is in the microwave, in a small bowl mix together the lemon juice with the icing/confectioners' sugar to make a drizzle.

As soon as the mug cake is out of the microwave put the drizzle in the microwave and heat for 20 seconds at 800W.

Prick the mug cake all over with a skewer or toothpick, hold the mug over the sink, and carefully pour the warmed drizzle over the top of the cake. At this point you can also pour over the optional almond liqueur.

Leave the mug cake to cool for 3 minutes before eating.

After-dinner mint mug cake

PREPARE: 2 MINUTES MICROWAVE: **1 MINUTE 50 SECONDS** COOL: **3 MINUTES**

*60 g/2 oz. dark/bittersweet
   chocolate*
2 tablespoons unsalted butter
1 teaspoon cocoa powder
2 tablespoons whole milk
1 UK medium/US large egg
*3 tablespoons self-raising/
   rising flour*
a pinch of salt
*2 tablespoons caster/
   granulated sugar*
*1/2 teaspoon peppermint
   extract*
*after-dinner mint crisps,
   broken into pieces to
   decorate*

a microwavable mug

MAKES 1

Chocolate fondant desserts are delicious, but can be quite tricky
to make. With a moist chocolate sponge and a puddle of rich
mint-flavoured chocolate at the bottom, you can whip up this mug
cake equivalent in a fraction of the time! Serve with your choice
of after-dinner mints on top – I like after-dinner mint crisps,
speckled with crunchy bits.

Chop half of the dark/bittersweet chocolate into small pieces
and add it to the mug along with the butter. Set the remaining
chocolate aside.

Microwave the contents of the mug for 20–30 seconds at 800W until
the chocolate has melted. Stir the melted chocolate and butter to
combine. Add the cocoa powder, then the milk and stir again until
smooth. Using a fork, beat in the egg until fully combined.

Add the flour, salt and sugar, and mix thoroughly until you
have a smooth batter. Pour in the peppermint extract and mix
thoroughly. Break the remaining chocolate into pieces and
drop into the centre of the unbaked mug cake. Top with
1 tablespoon of water and you're ready to microwave.

Microwave for 1 minute 50 seconds at 800W.
The cake will rise and then sink a little and
should still be quite wet to touch.

Leave the mug cake to cool for
3 minutes. Garnish with broken
after-dinner mints and enjoy!

Caffè latte mug cake

PREPARE: 2 MINUTES   MICROWAVE: **1 MINUTE 50 SECONDS**   COOL: **3 MINUTES**

2 tablespoons unsalted butter

1 tablespoon Irish cream
   liqueur

25 g/1 oz. white chocolate,
   chopped into small pieces

2 teaspoons instant coffee
   (dissolved in 1 tablespoon
   boiling water)

2 tablespoons caster/
   granulated sugar

1 UK medium/US large egg

4 tablespoons self-raising/
   rising flour

cocoa powder, to dust

a large microwavable mug

MAKES 1

Sometimes you fancy a cake and a coffee and here you can have both in one delicious mug cake! The Irish cream liqueur is a necessary drop of indulgence to give the cake its creamy flavour.

Add the butter, Irish cream liqueur and white chocolate to the mug and microwave for 20–30 seconds at 800W until the chocolate has melted.

Stir the dissolved coffee, add it into the mug and stir until smooth.

Add the sugar and mix thoroughly.

Using a fork, beat in the egg until fully combined.

Pour in the flour and mix until you have a batter – making sure to check all around the sides of the mug for any unmixed flour.

Put the mug on a plate as this is a very liquid batter and may well drip a bit down the sides of the mug while cooking. Microwave for 1 minute 50 seconds at 800W. The cake will rise a lot, then sink and should still be quite wet to touch.

Leave the mug cake to cool for 3 minutes and dust with cocoa powder before eating.

Caramel banana mug cake

PREPARE: **2 MINUTES** MICROWAVE: **2 MINUTES 40 SECONDS** COOL: **3 MINUTES**

1 medium (very ripe) banana
1 tablespoon porridge oats
$^1/_4$ teaspoon ground cinnamon
a generous pinch of salt
1 UK medium/US large egg
2 tablespoons light brown
  sugar
1 tablespoon vegetable oil
3 tablespoons self-raising/
  rising flour
2 tablespoons canned
  caramel

TO SERVE
1 tablespoon dark rum
  (optional)
canned caramel/dulce de
  leche
banana slices
ground cinnamon

a large microwavable mug
MAKES 1

Caramel and banana are a match made in heaven! Make sure you use a very ripe banana as this will give the cake lots of flavour and will also help to keep it moist long after it has baked. For an extra treat, top with dark rum as soon as the cake is out of the microwave.

In a small bowl, mash the banana with a fork.

Add the porridge oats, cinnamon and salt, and stir.

Put the egg and sugar into the mug, then whisk together using a fork.

Empty the banana mixture into the mug and mix well.

Stir in the oil.

Add the flour and mix thoroughly until you have a batter which will be lumpy because of the banana. Swirl in the caramel.

Put the mug on a plate in case any of the caramel leaks and microwave for 2 minutes 40 seconds at 800W. The cake will rise, then sink a little and should still be a little wet to touch.

As soon as the cake is out of the microwave, top with rum. Either way leave the mug cake to cool for 3 minutes because the caramel will be very hot.

To serve, drizzle with caramel, top with slices of banana and dust with cinnamon.

NOTE: The banana in this cake keeps it moist longer than most other mug cakes.

Mug cakes for family fun

Double chocolate brownie mug cake

PREPARE: **2 MINUTES** MICROWAVE: **1 MINUTE** COOL: **10 MINUTES**

2 tablespoons vegetable oil

1¹/₂ tablespoons cocoa powder

a pinch of salt

3 tablespoons caster/ granulated sugar

1 UK medium/US large egg

2 tablespoons plain/ all-purpose flour

a pinch of baking powder

1 tablespoon white chocolate chips

1 tablespoon milk/semi-sweet chocolate chips

vanilla ice cream, to serve

a tea cup or small microwavable mug

MAKES 1

This dense chocolate brownie is the perfect chocolate fix in a mug cake! If you prefer your brownies fudgier, then wait 10 minutes before eating. If you can't wait that long, then expect a gooey, softer, cake-like brownie. Perhaps try both ways at once to decide which way is best!

Mix together the oil and cocoa in the mug, until you have a thick chocolatey liquid.

Add in the salt and sugar, and stir thoroughly until smooth.

Using a fork, beat in the egg until fully combined.

Carefully stir in the flour and baking powder, making sure both are completely incorporated.

Fold in both the white and milk/semi-sweet chocolate chips.

Microwave for 1 minute at 800W. The cake will rise, then sink a little and should still be quite wet to touch. It also may well drip a little down the sides of the cup.

Leave the mug cake to cool for 10 minutes before eating if you prefer a fudgier brownie like me. Serve with a scoop of vanilla ice cream on top.

Chocolate orange marble mug cake

PREPARE: 3 MINUTES **MICROWAVE: 1 MINUTE 30 SECONDS** **COOL: 1 MINUTE**

Marble cake is as delicious to eat as it is fun to look at! Here you can make the quickest and easiest marble cake in a mug cake version.

In a bowl, beat together the oil, egg, sugar and flour until smooth.

Pour roughly half the mixture into another bowl.

To one of the bowls add the orange zest and juice, and mix together.

To the other bowl add the cocoa, cream and salt, and stir thoroughly.

Into the mug, drop alternate teaspoons of the orange mixture and the chocolate mixture, until you have used up all of both.

Microwave for 1 minute 30 seconds at 800W. The cake will rise, and should still be quite wet to touch. (It also may well drip a little down the sides of the mug as it is such a moist batter.)

Leave the mug cake to cool for 1 minute before eating and decorate with a little extra orange zest.

3 tablespoons vegetable oil

1 UK medium/US large egg

3 tablespoons caster/ granulated sugar

5 tablespoons self-raising/ rising flour

zest of $\frac{1}{2}$ medium orange, plus extra to decorate

1 teaspoon orange juice

$\frac{1}{2}$ tablespoon cocoa powder

1 teaspoon double/heavy cream

a pinch of salt

a microwavable mug

MAKES 1

Crushed-up cookie mug cake

PREPARE: 2 MINUTES MICROWAVE: **1 MINUTE 50 SECONDS** COOL: **3 MINUTES**

For all of those times when you just fancy some warm cookies and milk, here you have all of those flavours in a creamy, cookie-filled mug cake!

Add the butter and chopped white chocolate to a large mug and microwave for 20–30 seconds at 800W until the chocolate has melted.

Stir the melted chocolate and butter, add the cream and vanilla, and stir again until smooth.

Add in the sugar and mix thoroughly.

Using a fork, beat in the egg until fully combined.

Empty in the flour and mix well until you have a smooth batter.

Crush up the cookies and fold them into the mixture, making sure they are completely covered.

Microwave for 1 minute 50 seconds at 800W. The cake will rise, then sink a little and should still be quite wet to touch. (It also may well drip a little down the sides of the mug as it is such a moist batter.) Some of the cookies may also poke out of the cake!

Leave the mug cake to cool for 3 minutes before topping with more crushed cookies and eating.

2 tablespoons unsalted butter
20 g/³/₄ oz. white chocolate, chopped into small pieces
2 tablespoons double/heavy cream
1 teaspoon vanilla extract
2 tablespoons caster/ granulated sugar
1 UK medium/US large egg
4 tablespoons self-raising/ rising flour
3 store-bought small chocolate chip cookies, plus extra crumbs to decorate

a large microwavable mug

MAKES 1

Doughnut-stuffed mug cake

PREPARE: 2 MINUTES **MICROWAVE: 1 MINUTE 50 SECONDS** **COOL: 3 MINUTES**

*3 tablespoons double/heavy
   cream*
*25 g/1 oz. dark/bittersweet
   chocolate, chopped into
   small pieces*
1 UK medium/US large egg
*1 tablespoon caster/
   granulated sugar*
1 sugared or glazed doughnut

a small microwavable mug

MAKES 1

Breathe life into day-old doughnuts by turning them into this terrifically trashy tea-time treat! Chocolate, cream and doughnuts are all you really need for the perfect dessert.

Pour the cream into the mug then warm in the microwave for 20–30 seconds at 800W until hot.

Add the chocolate to the mug and stir until fully melted.

In a small bowl, whisk together the egg and sugar until fully mixed.

Pour the egg mixture into the mug and stir thoroughly.

Break the doughnuts into small pieces and place the pieces in the mug, carefully pushing them into the mixture to make sure they are fully covered. Move the doughnuts around so they are not flattened, as when the cake is microwaved it will be rise a lot, but then deflate back to a similar position that it went in at.

Microwave for 1 minute 50 seconds at 800W. The cake will rise, then sink and should still be quite wet to touch. (It also may well drip a little down the sides of the mug as it is such a moist batter).

Leave to cool for 3 minutes before eating.

Cookie cheats

Ice-cream cookies

PREPARE: **15 MINUTES** REFRIGERATE: **AT LEAST 1 HOUR (OR OVERNIGHT)**
BAKE: **10 MINUTES**

100 g/7 tablespoons unsalted butter, melted
110 g/^{1}/$_2$ cup plus 2 tablespoons caster/granulated sugar
1^1/$_2$ teaspoons vanilla extract
90 g/3 oz. vanilla ice cream, softened for 20 seconds in the microwave
250 g/1^3/$_4$ cups self-raising/rising flour
50 g/^{1}/$_3$ cup white chocolate chips
50 g/^{1}/$_4$ cup multi-coloured cake sprinkles
35 g/2 tablespoons chocolate sprinkles

2 baking sheets lined with baking parchment

MAKES 16

Soft vanilla cookies that use a scoop of your favourite ice cream in the dough are the perfect cookie to make when you don't have any eggs, but you do have ice cream!

Add the melted butter, sugar, vanilla extract and softened vanilla ice cream to the bowl of a free-standing mixer or a large mixing bowl with a handheld electric whisk. Mix together until all the ingredients are combined.

Gradually add in the flour, a quarter at a time, mixing well after each addition, until you have a sticky cookie dough.

Carefully fold in the white chocolate chips and both types of sprinkles until evenly distributed.

Pop the dough in the fridge to chill for at least an hour or overnight.

15 minutes before you remove the dough from the fridge, preheat the oven to 180°C (350°F) Gas 4.

Roll the dough into balls, flatten them slightly and space them out on the lined baking sheets.

Bake in batches for about 10 minutes until golden brown around the edges.

Leave them on the baking sheets for 2 minutes to harden, then carefully transfer to a wire rack to cool completely.

NOTE These cookies are best eaten on the day they are made, but can be stored for up to 3 days in an airtight container at room temperature.

Molten salted caramel chocolate chip cookie pots

PREPARE: 10 MINUTES BAKE: **18–20 MINUTES** COOL: **10 MINUTES**

90 g/6 tablespoons unsalted
   butter
125 g/²/₃ cup caster/
   granulated sugar
75 g/¹/₃ cup light brown sugar
1 teaspoon vanilla extract
1 UK large/US extra-large egg
225 g/1²/₃ cups self-raising/
   rising flour
100 g/²/₃ cup dark/bittersweet
   chocolate chips
12 tablespoons canned
   caramel/dulce de leche
salt, to sprinkle

6 ramekins, approximately
   8 x 4 cm/3¹/₂ x 1³/₄ inch

a baking sheet

MAKES 6

With these cookie pots you have a chewy chocolate chip cookie-topped dessert hiding a liquid caramel centre. This recipe is the reason we have the saying 'always leave room for dessert!'

Preheat the oven to 180°C (350°F) Gas 4.

In the bowl of a free-standing mixer or in a large mixing bowl with a handheld electric whisk, beat together the butter, both sugars and vanilla extract until light and fluffy.

Add the egg and mix until incorporated.

Add half of the flour, mix together well, then add the other half and mix well.

Stir in the chocolate chips by hand until they are evenly distributed.

Split the dough into 2 portions and set one half aside.

Split the dough you are using into 3 portions, then halve each portion. You should be left with 6 roughly equal portions and half of the original dough set aside.

Roll the 6 dough portions into balls, flatten them slightly, then press each of them into a ramekin. Top the middle of each cookie base with 2 tablespoons of caramel and a pinch of salt.

Repeat this process with the remaining dough. Roll the 6 dough portions into balls, flatten them slightly, then carefully place them on top of the caramel in each ramekin, pressing around the edges to seal the caramel inside.

Bake in the preheated oven for 18–20 minutes until the cookie top is golden brown, but the pot still has a bit of a wobble. (You may want to pop a baking sheet at the bottom of your oven to catch any cookie bits that may break off while baking.)

Leave to cool for 10 minutes before eating.

NOTE These pots are best eaten on the day they are made. They can be refrigerated for up to a day before baking.

Cookie-stuffed cookies

PREPARE: **15 MINUTES** REFRIGERATE: **AT LEAST 2 HOURS (OR OVERNIGHT)** BAKE: **10–14 MINUTES**

What is better than a homemade cookie? A homemade cookie with your favourite store-bought cookie baked inside of course!

Cream together the butter and both sugars in the bowl of a free-standing mixer or in a large mixing bowl with a handheld electric whisk.

Into a separate bowl, measure in the dry ingredients: flour, cocoa powder, salt and bicarbonate of soda/baking soda. Stir to combine.

Into the first bowl, add an egg and a third of the dry mixture. Mix until incorporated.

Add the next egg, with another third of the dry ingredients and mix.

Add in the final egg and the final third of the dry ingredients and mix until you have a soft, sticky dough.

Fold in the white chocolate chips until evenly distributed.

Pop the bowl in the fridge to chill for at least 2 hours (or overnight).

15 minutes before you remove the dough from the fridge, preheat the oven to 180°C (350°F) Gas 4.

Use an ice-cream scoop to portion the dough. Make one ball, flatten it and place a store-bought cookie on top. Make another ball with the ice-cream scoop, flatten it and place it on top of the store-bought cookie. Seal the edges of the homemade cookie dough, making sure there are no gaps. Gently place the cookie parcel onto the prepared baking sheet and push down on it slightly, being careful not to press down too hard as this could break the bought cookie inside. Repeat this process and space the cookies out on the baking sheets.

Bake the cookies in batches in the preheated oven for 10–14 minutes until puffed up. (Put any 'waiting' unbaked cookies in the fridge while other batches are baking.)

Once baked, remove from the sheet and place on a wire rack to cool. The cookies can be eaten warm, but once cooled, the cookie inside will harden.

NOTE These cookies are best eaten once they are cool, on the day they are made, but can be stored for up to 3 days in an airtight container at room temperature.

150 g/1 stick plus 2 tablespoons unsalted butter

150 g/³/₄ cup light brown sugar

200 g/1 cup caster/granulated sugar

450 g/3¹/₃ cups plain/all-purpose flour

50 g/¹/₂ cup cocoa powder

a pinch of salt

1¹/₂ teaspoons bicarbonate of soda/baking soda

3 UK large/US extra-large eggs

150 g/scant 1 cup white chocolate chips

10 of your favourite store-bought cookies (I use Chips Ahoy)

2–3 baking sheets lined with baking parchment

MAKES 10

S'mores cookie squares

PREPARE: **10 MINUTES** BAKE: **25 MINUTES**

120 g/1 stick unsalted butter

140 g/²/₃ cup light brown
   sugar

1 UK large/US extra-large egg
   plus 1 UK large/US
   extra-large egg yolk

1 teaspoon vanilla extract

300 g/2¹/₄ cups plain/
   all-purpose flour

¹/₂ teaspoon baking powder

a pinch of salt

150 g/1¹/₄ cups cookie crumbs
   (digestive biscuits/Graham
   crackers work well)

200 g/5 cups marshmallow
   fluff

100 g/²/₃ cup dark/bittersweet
   chocolate chips

100 g/²/₃ cup milk/semi-sweet
   chocolate chips

a 23-cm/9-inch square, deep
   baking pan, greased and
   lined with baking parchment

MAKES 16

Traditionally s'mores are a camp-fire treat of melted marshmallows and chocolate, sandwiched between Graham cracker cookies that are akin to digestive biscuits in the UK. These s'mores cookie squares recreate all the goodness of s'mores but without the need for a camp-fire!

Preheat the oven to 170°C (325°F) Gas 3

In the bowl of a free-standing mixer or in a large mixing bowl with a handheld electric whisk, beat together the butter and sugar until pale.

Add in the egg, egg yolk and vanilla extract, and mix until incorporated.

In a separate bowl, mix together the flour, baking powder, salt and 120 g/1 cup of the biscuit crumbs. Add one half of this mixture to the first bowl, mixing well before adding in the remaining half. Leave the remaining biscuit crumbs to one side.

You should now have a soft dough. Press two-thirds of the dough into the base of the prepared baking pan, making sure it is evenly spread.

Using a greased spoon and spatula, carefully spread the marshmallow fluff across the cookie base. (This is easiest to do when you drop small amounts of fluff all over the base and spread with the spatula.)

Sprinkle both the chocolate chips all over the marshmallow.

Drop small pieces of the remaining cookie dough over the top of the chocolate chips, until you have used all of the dough up.

Finally, sprinkle the remaining cookie crumbs over the top .

Bake in the preheated oven for about 25 minutes until the cookie top is golden brown and it is still quite soft – this may take a few minutes longer depending on your oven.

Leave to cool completely before slicing into squares and eating.

NOTE These cookies can be stored for up to 5 days in an airtight container at room temperature.

Garbage cookies

PREPARE: 15 MINUTES BAKING: 8–10 MINUTES

Don't be put off by the name, Garbage Cookies are in fact cookies that are full of all things good! Oats, Rice Krispies, M&M's, pretzels, potato chips and chocolate chips all generously baked into a soft doughy cookie. They're the ultimate trashy cookie and they taste deliciously naughty! Just make sure you wait until they've completely cooled before eating them as this gives the pretzels a chance to re-harden and gives the cookies the perfect salty crunch.

Preheat the oven to 180°C (350°F) Gas 4.

Cream together the butter and both sugars in the bowl of a free-standing mixer or in a large mixing bowl with a handheld electric whisk.

Add in the egg and egg yolk, and mix until fully combined.

Gradually add in the flour until you have a sticky cookie dough.

Fold in the oats and Rice Krispies by hand.

Add in the M&M's, crushed pretzels, crushed potato chips and both chocolate chips. Use your hands to bring the dough together and make sure all of the additions are evenly distributed throughout.

Use an ice-cream scoop to portion the cookies, then roll them in your hands, before flattening them slightly and spacing well apart on the lined baking sheets.

Bake the cookies in batches in the preheated oven for 8–10 minutes until light golden brown on the edges.

Leave the cookies to cool for 2 minutes on the baking sheets before carefully removing them and transferring them to a wire rack to cool completely.

Wait until they are completely cool before eating.

NOTE These cookies are best eaten once they are cool, on the day they are made, but can be stored for up to 3 days in an airtight container at room temperature.

100 g/7 tablespoons unsalted butter

100 g/¹/₂ cup light brown sugar

125 g/²/₃ cup caster/ granulated sugar

1 UK large/US extra-large egg plus 1 UK large/US extra-large egg yolk

200 g/1¹/₂ cups self-raising/ rising flour

40 g/¹/₂ cup porridge oats

20 g/1 cup puffed rice cereal (I use Rice Krispies)

100 g/²/₃ cup M&M's

30 g/1 cup pretzels, crushed

30 g/1 cup lightly salted potato chips, crushed

65 g/¹/₂ cup dark/bittersweet chocolate chips

50 g/¹/₃ cup white chocolate chips

2–3 baking sheets lined with baking parchment

MAKES 18

Cream cheese coffee cake muffins

PREPARE: **15 MINUTES** BAKE: **20 MINUTES**

250 g/2 cups self-raising/
rising flour
225 g/1 cup plus 2
tablespoons caster/
granulated sugar
a pinch of salt
1 teaspoon ground cinnamon
150 g/1 stick plus 2
tablespoons unsalted
butter, at room temperature
2 UK large/US extra-large
eggs
150 g/³/4 cup full-fat cream
cheese, at room
temperature
100 g/¹/2 cup light brown
sugar

a 12-hole muffin pan lined with
large paper cases

MAKES 12

American coffee cake is traditionally a soft, cinnamon-spiced cake with a crunchy streusel topping that is served with a cup of coffee, but doesn't actually have any coffee in it. The addition of cream cheese makes these muffins beautifully light.

Preheat the oven to 180°C (350°F) Gas 4.

In a large bowl, using your hands, carefully combine the flour, caster/granulated sugar, salt, cinnamon and butter until you have a sandy texture.

Take out 120 g/4 oz. of this mixture and set it aside in a small bowl (this will form part of the crumb topping later).

Into the bowl, add the eggs and cream cheese, and beat just until you have a smooth cake batter.

Into the small bowl, add the light brown sugar and carefully mix but don't worry if there are still lumps – lumps are good for a crumb topping!

Using an ice-cream scoop, fill the muffin cases with the cake batter.

Sprinkle the crumb topping over each muffin, make sure the entire surface is covered and lightly push the topping into the muffin.

Bake in the preheated oven for about 20 minutes until each muffin is golden brown. (Some of the topping will fall off during baking, but this is normal.)

Once baked, remove from the oven and allow them to cool in the pan for about 5 minutes, before transferring to a wire rack. These muffins are delicious served hot, straight from the oven.

NOTE These muffins are best eaten on the day they are made, but can be stored for up to 3 days in an airtight container at room temperature.

Soda pop dump cake

PREPARE: **5 MINUTES** BAKE: **30–40 MINUTES**

300 g/2¹/₂ cups fresh
  blueberries
150 g/¹/₂ cup blueberry
  jam/jelly, plus extra to serve
1 box vanilla cake mix
1 can clear, sprakling
  lemonade, such as Sprite
whipped cream, to serve

a 30 x 18 x 4-cm/
  11 x 7 x 1¹/₂-inch cake pan

SERVES 12

Dump cakes are literally cakes where you can dump all of the ingredients in a cake pan and let the oven work its magic. The key ingredient for a dump cake is a boxed cake mix and with this recipe the trashiness is upped by adding a can of Sprite, too! This is possibly the easiest cake you will ever make.

Preheat the oven to 180°C (350°F) Gas 4.

Empty the blueberries into the bottom of the cake pan (no need to grease the pan).

Dollop spoonfuls of jam/jelly over the blueberries.

In a separate bowl, whisk together the cake mix and Sprite. It will foam and still be a bit lumpy, but that is normal.

Pour the cake batter over the blueberries and jam/jelly and make sure it covers the whole pan. Don't worry if some of the jam/jelly leaks into the batter – that adds deliciousness!

Bake in the preheated oven for 30–40 minutes until the top of the cake is golden brown and it is springy to the touch.

Serve immediately with whipped cream and more blueberry jam/jelly on top.

NOTE This cake is best eaten warm on the day it is made.

TIP You could melt the blueberry jam/jelly in a saucepan over low heat to drizzle over the top but dolloping more on top of warm cake will work just as well.

Candy bar-stuffed croissants

PREPARE: **15 MINUTES** SOAK: **AT LEAST 2 HOURS (OR OVERNIGHT)**
BAKE: **40–50 MINUTES**

Not only is this chocolate-filled, buttery croissant and custard delight absolutely scrumptious to eat, it is also a brilliant 'make it all ahead and just pop it in the oven when it's nearly time for dessert' dessert. Minimum effort, maximum yumminess!

5 slightly stale croissants
unsalted butter, for spreading
    and topping
5 chocolate/candy bars (all
    the same or different is fine)
300 ml/1¹⁄₃ cups double/heavy
    cream
300 ml/1¹⁄₂ cups whole milk
200 g/1 cup caster/granulated
    sugar
3 UK large/US extra-large
    eggs
2 teaspoons white sugar

a 22 x 17 x 6-cm/9 x 7 x 2-inch
    cake pan

SERVES 8

Slice through the croissants, but stop just short of cutting all of the way through, so that one side is still attached.

Butter each croissant centre.

Fill each croissant with a chocolate/candy bar of your choice.

In a large bowl, whisk together the cream, milk, caster/granulated sugar and eggs until fully incorporated.

Carefully dip each croissant sandwich into the liquid before laying them in the cake pan, cut-side down. You should be able to fit all 5 croissants in, one next to the other.

Pour the liquid mixture over the top of the croissants, cover with clingfilm/plastic wrap and pop the dish in the fridge for at least 2 hours – overnight is better.

30 minutes before you are ready to bake, remove the dessert from the fridge.

15 minutes before you are ready to bake, preheat the oven to 180°C (350°F) Gas 4.

Dot the top of the dessert with a few small knobs of butter, sprinkle with the white sugar and bake in the preheated oven for 40–50 minutes until golden brown and the custard mixture has set.

Wait 5 minutes before serving and eating.

NOTE This dessert is best eaten on the day it is made.

Apple pie pastry pockets

PREPARE: 25 MINUTES BAKE: 12–15 MINUTES

2 medium Granny Smith
apples, peeled, cored and
chopped into small cubes
1 teaspoon lemon juice
50 g/¼ cup light brown sugar
1 teaspoon ground cinnamon
50 g/⅔ cup cookie crumbs
(digestive biscuits/Graham
crackers work well)
1 rectangular sheet of
ready-made puff pastry
dough (approximately 33 x
23 cm/ 13 x 9 inches)
plain/all-purpose flour, for
dusting
1 UK large/US extra-large egg
yolk mixed with
2 tablespoons water
25 g/2 tablespoons white
sugar
½ teaspoon ground cinnamon
vanilla ice cream or cream,
to serve

a baking sheet lined with
baking parchment

SERVES 4

Warm apple pie is the ultimate comfort food. Using store-bought puff pastry makes them super easy and as these are individual portions, you never have to share!

Put the apple cubes in a saucepan and set over a medium heat, along with the lemon juice, sugar, cinnamon and 1 tablespoon of water.

Cover the saucepan with a lid and leave for 15 minutes until the liquid is thick and bubbling and the apples are just soft.

Meanwhile, preheat the oven to 200°C (400°F) Gas 6.

Once the 15 minutes are up, empty the apple mixture into a bowl and mix with the cookie crumbs. Set this mixture aside to cool a little further.

Unroll the puff pastry dough onto a floured worksurface and using a pizza cutter or knife, cut it into 8 even rectangles. Arrange 4 pastry rectangles on the lined baking sheet.

Spoon a quarter of the apple mixture onto the middle of these pastry rectangles using all of the mixture. Make sure the edges of the pastry are free of apple.

Using a pastry brush or your finger, brush the edges of the apple-topped pastry rectangles with the egg yolk and water mixture.

Place a pastry 'lid' on top of each apple-topped pastry rectangle, gently pressing the edges together. Use a fork to press the edges together further and to decorate around all of the sides. Using a sharp knife, make three slits across the middle of the pastry pocket and brush with the egg wash all over the top.

In a small bowl mix together the white sugar and cinnamon and sprinkle this mixture over the top of each pie.

Bake in the preheated oven for 12–15 minutes until puffed up and golden.

Serve immediately with vanilla ice cream or cream.

NOTE These pies are best eaten warm, on the day they are made. They can be stored un-baked for a day in the fridge. Egg wash them and sprinkle with cinnamon sugar just before baking.

Turtle brownie bites

PREPARE: 20 MINUTES **BAKE: 18–20 MINUTES**

140 g/1 stick plus 1¹/₂
   tablespoons unsalted butter
140 g/5 oz. dark/bittersweet
   chocolate
200 g/1 cup caster/granulated
   sugar
100 g/³/₄ cup plain/all-purpose
   flour
a pinch of salt
2 UK large/US extra-large eggs
50 g/¹/₂ cup chopped pecans

TOPPING:

12 chewy caramels in milk/
   semi-sweet chocolate
   (I use Rolo)
50 g/2 oz. melted dark/
   bittwersweet chocolate
20 g/scant ¹/₄ cup chopped
   pecans

a muffin pan, greased

These brownie bites take their inspiration from the popular American candy 'Turtles', which consist of chocolate, caramel and pecans. For the gooey caramel middle of these brownie bites, pop a Rolo into the centre when it has just come out of the oven.

Preheat your oven to 170°C (325°F) Gas 3.

In a large saucepan, melt the butter over a medium heat.

Once melted, take the pan off the heat and add the chocolate to the melted butter. Stir and set aside. Once the chocolate has completed melted, pour the sugar into the pan and stir thoroughly.

Add the flour to the mixture, along with the salt and stir until it is all incorporated.

Add one egg at a time, mixing well after each addition, until you have a thick brownie batter.

Fold in the chopped pecans, making sure they are spread throughout.

Using an ice-cream scoop, fill the muffin pan with the brownie batter. You should have just enough to fill a 12-hole pan.

Bake in the preheated oven for 18–20 minutes until the tops have a papery look and they still have a bit of a wobble! Don't worry if the tops crack a bit, that is supposed to happen!

As soon as you have removed the pan from the oven, push a Rolo into the centre of each brownie bite.

Run a palette knife around the edge of each brownie to loosen them from the pan, but leave the brownie bites to cool completely in the pan before removing.

Once removed, drizzle the melted chocolate across the top of them and sprinkle with the chopped pecans.

NOTE These brownie bites can be stored for up to 5 days in an airtight container at room temperature.

No-bake bakes

Individual no-bake cookie butter cheesecakes

PREPARE: **15 MINUTES** REFRIGERATE: **AT LEAST 3 HOURS (OR OVERNIGHT)**

100 g/3¹/₂ oz. cookies
 (digestive biscuits/Graham
 crackers work well)
25 g/1³/₄ tablespoons unsalted
 butter
¹/₂ teaspoon ground cinnamon
1 teaspoon light brown sugar
350 g/1³/₄ cups full-fat cream
 cheese
200 g/1 cup cookie butter,
 such as Biscoff or
 Speculoos
150 ml/³/₄ cup double/heavy
 cream
80 g/¹/₂ cup icing/
 confectioners' sugar, sifted

TO SERVE
cookie crumbs
4 whole cookies

4 glass dessert bowls, sundae
 glasses or ramekins

MAKES 4

No-bake cheesecakes are the ideal way to get your cheesecake fix without the need for baking. Cookie butter works brilliantly to flavour this cheesecake and is also delicious eaten with a spoon directly from the jar!

In a food processor, blitz the cookies until they resemble fine breadcrumbs. Alternatively, put them in a food bag, wrap in a clean kitchen cloth and bash with the end of a rolling pin.

Melt the butter in the microwave for 20–30 seconds at 800W.

Pour the melted butter, cinnamon and light brown sugar into the food processor and pulse until all of the cookie crumbs are wet. Alternatively mix well with a wooden spoon in a large mixing bowl.

Spoon the cookie crumbs into the serving bowls, so that each bowl has an equal amount. Use a teaspoon to push the crumbs in and to give them a flat surface.

Into the bowl of a free-standing mixer with a whisk attachment or a mixing bowl using a handheld electric whisk, empty in the cream cheese and cookie butter and whip until fully combined and pale. Pour in the cream and sifted icing/confectioners' sugar and whip again on a medium speed for 2–3 minutes until thickened.

Spoon the cheesecake mixture on top of the cookie bases, so that each bowl has an equal amount, then put in the fridge for at least 3 hours (or overnight).

Just before serving, top with cookie crumbs and a whole cookie.

NOTE These cheesecakes should be stored in the fridge and eaten within 3 days.

Cheat's peanut butter fudge

PREPARE: **10 MINUTES** REFRIGERATE: **AT LEAST 4 HOURS (OR OVERNIGHT)**

500 g/2¼ cups smooth
   peanut butter (you want the
   least oily peanut butter that
   you can find)
1 x 397-g/14-oz. can
   sweetened condensed milk
a pinch of salt
100 g/²⁄₃ cup icing/
   confectioners' sugar, sifted
100 g/²⁄₃ cup dark/bittersweet
   chocolate chips
100 g/1 cup chopped peanuts

a 28 x 18 x 4-cm /11 x 7 x
   1.5-inch cake pan, lined
   with overhanging baking
   parchment

MAKES 64 PIECES

This is an easy fudge recipe without the need for any sugar thermometers at all.
The hard part is only eating one piece – for me, it's impossible!

In a large saucepan, melt together the peanut butter, condensed milk and salt over a medium heat.

Remove the saucepan from the heat and stir to loosen the mixture.

Carefully add in the sifted icing/confectioners' sugar and stir until fully combined and very thick.

Empty the mixture into the prepared cake pan, making sure it covers the whole of the base – the weight of the mixture will hold down the baking parchment. It will be quite oily and you will need to use the back of a spoon to smooth the fudge out.

Sprinkle over the dark chocolate chips, making sure they are spread out and push them in to the fudge slightly. They may melt a little but this is okay.

Sprinkle over the chopped peanuts, pushing them in to the fudge, too.

Allow the fudge to cool, then pop it in to the fridge to set for at least 4 hours or overnight.

Once set, use the overhanging baking parchment to lift the fudge out of the pan.

Slice the fudge into small squares and enjoy.

NOTE You can store this fudge for around 2 weeks in an airtight container in the fridge, but it is best eaten at room temperature.

Cookies and cream ice-box cake

PREPARE: **20 MINUTES** REFRIGERATE: **AT LEAST 5 HOURS (OR OVERNIGHT)**

Ice-box cakes consist of cookies and cream sandwiched together and then put in the fridge, so that the cream softens the cookies and turns them 'cake-like'. Some recipes use whole cookies and some use crushed cookies. This recipe uses both because you can never have too many Oreos!

Into the bowl of a free-standing mixer with a whisk attachment or a mixing bowl with a handheld electric whisk, empty in the cream, sugar and vanilla extract, and whip until you have stiff peaks (5–7 minutes).

Meanwhile, using a food processor, crush 14 of the Oreo cookies until you have crumbs. Alternatively, put them in a food bag, wrap in a clean kitchen cloth and bash with the end of a rolling pin.

Once the cream has been whipped, divide it into equally into 4 portions.

Empty one portion of cream into the bottom of the cake pan and spread it out so that it covers the entire base. Take 16 Oreos, dip each side in milk, before placing them on top of the cream in equal rows of 4 cookies. Sprinkle a large handful of the cookie crumbs over any cream that isn't covered by the cookies, concentrating on the edges.

Empty another portion of cream on top of the Oreos and spread it out with teaspoons so that the top is entirely covered – don't worry if cookie crumbs mix into the cream.

Take another 16 Oreos, dip each side in milk, and place them on top of the cream in equal rows of 4 cookies. Once again sprinkle a large handful of the cookie crumbs over any cream that isn't covered by the whole cookies.

Repeat this process one more time – cream and then cookies.

When ready, empty the final portion of cream on top of the Oreos and spread it out with a teaspoon so that it covers the entire top. Sprinkle the rest of the Oreo crumbs all over the top of the cream. Break the remaining 8 Oreos into chunks and stick them into the cream so they look like little shards. Cover the pan with clingfilm/plastic wrap and put it in the fridge to chill for at least 5 hours, or overnight.

Slice into squares, drizzle with chocolate sauce and serve.

NOTE This dessert is best stored in the fridge and eaten within 3 days.

*800 ml/3³/₄ cups double/
heavy cream*
*50 g/¹/₃ cup icing/
confectioners' sugar*
1 tablespoon vanilla extract
70 Oreo cookies
150 ml/³/₄ cup whole milk
chocolate sauce, to serve

a 23 x 23 x 5-cm/
9 x 9 x 2-inch cake pan

MAKES 16

Breakfast cereal bars

PREPARE: 15 MINUTES COOLING TIME: **AT LEAST 1 HOUR**

*40 g/2¹/₂ tablespoons
   unsalted butter*
200 g/7 oz. white chocolate
*200 g/5 cups mini white
   marshmallows*
*250 g/10 cups of your
   favourite breakfast cereals
   (a combination of 3–4
   different kinds works best
   – I like Lucky Charms,
   Cheerios, Cornflakes and
   Rice Krispies)*
30 g/2 tablespoons sprinkles

a 33 x 23 x 5-cm/13 x 9 x
   2-inch cake pan, greased

MAKES 32

By adding butter, white chocolate and marshmallows to your favourite breakfast cereals, you can have 'breakfast' all day long!

Melt the butter in a very large saucepan over a medium heat.

Chop the chocolate into small pieces and once the butter has melted, add the chocolate to the saucepan still on the heat.

Once the chocolate has melted, add in the marshmallows. At first the chocolate will form a paste around the marshmallows, but as the marshmallows melt, the whole mixture will come together into a pale yellow thick, marshmallowy glue.

Once you have your marshmallow glue, take the pan off the heat and pour in the breakfast cereals. Work quickly to ensure that all of the cereal is coated.

Transfer the cereal mixture to the prepared cake pan and use the back of a spoon to make sure that the whole pan is filled. You can also use a sheet of baking parchment to push down on the mixture to make sure the top is flat.

Sprinkle the top with sprinkles and push them into the cereal using the baking parchment.

Cover the pan with clingfilm/plastic wrap and leave to set at room temperature for at least 1 hour before slicing.

NOTE These are best eaten on the day they are made but can be stored for up to 5 days in an airtight container at room temperature.

Popcorn overload rocky road

PREPARE: **15 MINUTES** REFRIGERATE: **AT LEAST 3 HOURS (OR OVERNIGHT)**

This sweet and salty rocky road overloaded with popcorn is an easy, no-bake treat to make with the kids. Make sure all of the ingredients end up in the rocky road though and not small tummies!

Melt the milk chocolate in a large bowl set over a pan of simmering water.

Into another large bowl, measure in both popcorns, the malted chocolate balls and mini marshmallows.

Carefully crush the pretzels and Oreo cookies, and add them to the large bowl of ingredients.

Once the chocolate has melted, take it off the heat and leave it cool slightly (for about 5 minutes).

After 5 minutes, pour the melted chocolate into the bowl of ingredients and carefully mix, ensuring that everything is coated with chocolate.

Transfer the mixture to the prepared cake pan and use the back of a spoon to make sure that the whole pan is filled.

Cover the top of the pan with clingfilm/plastic wrap and put in the fridge for at least 3 hours.

Remove the pan from the fridge and let it sit for 5 minutes before slicing.

NOTE These can be stored for up to 5 days in an airtight container at room temperature or in the fridge, but are best eaten at room temperature.

420 g/15 oz. milk/semi-sweet chocolate
65 g/2¼ oz. salted popcorn
100 g/3½ oz. toffee popcorn
75 g/3 oz. malted chocolate balls (Maltesers or Whoppers)
40 mini marshmallows
50 g/2 oz. pretzels
6 Oreo cookies

a 33 x 23 x 5-cm /13 x 9 x 2-inch cake pan, lined with overhanging clingfilm/plastic wrap

MAKES 32

Index

A
after-dinner mint mug cake 21
apple pie pastry pockets 50

B
bananas: caramel banana mug cake 25
berries: boozy berry mug cake 17
blueberries: soda pop dump cake 46
boozy berry mug cake 17
breakfast cereal bars 60
brownies: double chocolate brownie mug cake 27
    turtle brownie bites 53

C
caffè latte mug cake 22
candy bar-stuffed croissants 49
caramel: caramel banana mug cake 25
    molten salted caramel chocolate chip cookie pots 36
cereal bars, breakfast 60
cheat's peanut butter fudge 56
cheesecakes, no-bake cookie butter 55
chocolate: after-dinner mint mug cake 21
    breakfast cereal bars 60
    caffè latte mug cake 22
    candy bar-stuffed croissants 49
    cheat's peanut butter fudge 56
    chocolate orange marble mug cake 28
    cookie dough mug cake 13
    cookie-stuffed cookies 39
    cookies and cream ice-box cake 59
    crushed-up cookie mug cake 31
    double chocolate brownie mug cake 27
    doughnut-stuffed mug cake 32
    garbage cookies 43
    Oreo mug cake 14
    ice-cream cookies 35
    molten salted caramel chocolate chip cookie pots 36
    PB-Nutella mug cake 9
    popcorn overload rocky road 63
    s'mores cookie squares 40
    sprinkle sunshine mug cake 10
    turtle brownie bites 53
    white chocolate and lemon drizzle mug cake 18
coffee: caffè latte mug cake 22
condensed milk: cheat's peanut butter fudge 56
cookies: cookie dough mug cake 13
    cookie-stuffed cookies 39
    cookies and cream ice-box cake 59
    crushed-up cookie mug cake 31
    garbage cookies 43
    ice-cream cookies 35
    molten salted caramel chocolate chip cookie pots 36
    no-bake cookie butter cheesecakes 55
    s'mores cookie squares 40
cream: candy bar-stuffed croissants 49
    cookies and cream ice-box cake 59
    crushed-up cookie mug cake 31
    doughnut-stuffed mug cake 32
    no-bake cookie butter cheesecakes 55
cream cheese: cream cheese coffee cake muffins 45
    no-bake cookie butter cheesecakes 55
croissants, candy bar-stuffed 49
crushed-up cookie mug cake 31

D
doughnut-stuffed mug cake 32
dump cake, soda pop 46

F G
fudge, cheat's peanut butter 56
garbage cookies 43

H I
Oreo mug cake 14
ice-box cake, cookies and cream 59
ice-cream cookies 35
Irish cream: caffè latte mug cake 22

L M
lemons: white chocolate and lemon drizzle mug cake 18
marble mug cake, chocolate orange 28
marshmallows: breakfast cereal bars 60
    popcorn overload rocky road 63
    s'mores cookie squares 40
mint: after-dinner mint mug cake 21
molten salted caramel chocolate chip cookie pots 36
muffins, cream cheese coffee cake 45

N O
no-bake cookie butter cheesecakes 55
Nutella: PB-Nutella mug cake 9

oats: caramel banana mug cake 25
    garbage cookies 43
oranges: chocolate orange marble mug cake 28
Oreo cookies: cookies and cream ice-box cake 59
    Oreo mug cake 14
    popcorn overload rocky road 63

P
pastry pockets, apple pie 50

peanut butter: cheat's peanut butter fudge 56
    PB-Nutella mug cake 9
pecans: turtle brownie bites 53
popcorn overload rocky road 63
pretzels: garbage cookies 43
    popcorn overload rocky road 63
puffed rice cereal: garbage cookies 43

R
raspberry jam/jelly: boozy berry mug cake 17
rocky road, popcorn overload 63

S
salted caramel chocolate chip cookie pots, molten 36
s'mores cookie squares 40
soda pop dump cake 46
sprinkle sunshine mug cake 10

T V
turtle brownie bites 53
vanilla: sprinkle sunshine mug cake 10